T0023738

Take Note

ALSO BY TONI TONE

I Wish I Knew This Earlier: Lessons on Love

Take Note

Real Life Lessons

Toni Tone

4th ESTATE • *London*

4th Estate
An imprint of HarperCollins*Publishers*
1 London Bridge Street
London SE1 9GF

www.4thestate.co.uk

HarperCollins*Publishers*
Macken House, 39/40 Mayor Street Upper
Dublin1, D01 C9W8

First published in Great Britain in 2022 by 4th Estate

1

Copyright © Toni Tone 2022

Toni Tone asserts the moral right to be identified
as the author of this work in accordance with the
Copyright, Designs and Patents Act 1988

A catalogue record for this book is
available from the British Library

ISBN 978-0-00-855613-6

All rights reserved. No part of this publication may be
reproduced, stored in a retrieval system, or transmitted,
in any form or by any means, electronic, mechanical,
photocopying, recording or otherwise, without the
prior permission of the publishers.

This book is sold subject to the condition that it shall not, by
way of trade or otherwise, be lent, re-sold, hired out or otherwise
circulated without the publisher's prior consent in any form of
binding or cover other than that in which it is published and
without a similar condition including this condition being
imposed on the subsequent purchaser.

Set in Adobe Garamond Pro
Printed and bound in the UK using 100%
renewable electricity at CPI Group (UK) Ltd

MIX
Paper | Supporting
responsible forestry
FSC™ C007454
www.fsc.org

This book is produced from independently certified FSC™ paper
to ensure responsible forest management.

For more information visit: www.harpercollins.co.uk/green

*For Margaret Adenle and Rosemary Aregbesola –
my amazing grandmothers. You may no longer be with
us in person, but your spirit, your love and your impact
lives on. Thank you for everything.*

*To all the young women who need a little life guidance
right now, this book is also dedicated to you.*

Contents

Foreword

After releasing my debut book, *I Wish I Knew This Earlier: Lessons on Love*, I was inundated with requests for book two. I couldn't have predicted how successful my debut has been, but needless to say I was very pleased. If you've read my first book, you'll know that it is filled with numerous lessons on love – more specifically, lessons on dating, loving and healing. Once I had accepted that I wanted to write another book, I asked myself: 'What the hell am I going to share next?' – and that's when it dawned on me.

Although romantic love impacts us all in some way or other, it is just one aspect of our lives, and it's just one of the many things people approach me for advice on. Outside of romance, people struggle with their identity, their confidence, their friendships, their career, and so much more. In fact, all these are areas I have struggled with at some point. I concluded that this is exactly what I wanted to explore in book two: the challenges I faced in my twenties, which I learned from and managed to overcome. This book is filled with lessons that were a direct result of my decisions, my actions and my experiences. Lessons that have shaped me to be more confident, more productive and happier in general … I wanted to share my takeaways, my notes, my real life lessons. The lessons that I believe will bring you closer to reaching your full potential.

Within this book, I'm going to take you on a bit of a journey. I'm going to cover everything from feeling like you don't completely fit in, to feeling like you're behind everyone else in life. I'll explore the problem with overthinking, and the value of asking for help. I'll delve into outgrowing friendships and what makes a good friend. I'll highlight the importance of celebrating your successes, ways to work more efficiently, and so much more. I have chosen to touch on an array of different topics, with the aim of teaching you something new across more than one aspect of your life.

As you may be aware from my first book, I've found myself playing a big-sister role to plenty of people online. It wasn't even something I sought out to do. It just occurred naturally. It's a privilege I am grateful for, and it's partly why I wrote my first book to begin with. Keeping in line with *I Wish I Knew This Earlier*, I want to continue providing that sisterly advice. I have written *Take Note* as an accessible, insightful and easy-to-carry guide – one that you can read in the order that suits you best.

I hope to continue generating productive online conversations with *Take Note* too, and if you wish to get involved, please use the hashtag #TakeNoteLessons.

Section 1: Confidence and Identity

In all the work I do, there are a handful of topics that constantly reappear when it comes to offering up my advice and assistance to the people who follow me online. One of these topics is confidence. Whether it's during my talks or online Q&As, I'm often asked how to tackle low self-esteem and what I did to have confidence.

What many people don't know is that I haven't always been a confident person. As a child and teenager, I felt very awkward. My awkwardness was a product of believing I never truly belonged. I'm sure you know how it is when you're in school … There are cliques everywhere.

I was that person who floated in between these core groups. I'd have one best friend, but outside of that one person, I never felt like I belonged in any of the various groups in school. At the time I saw that as a weakness, but it has come to be a strength. Even as a thirty-something-year-old woman, my life mirrors my school years. I have one best friend, and I flutter in between different circles – but this time I understand that it's because I possess the versatility to do so comfortably – not because I don't 'belong'.

In this section of my book, I'm going to address some of the lessons I learned that helped me develop my own self-confidence and sense of identity. I want to stress that the road to feeling confident isn't a straight line. There are twists and there are turns, but the longer you walk the journey, the more equipped you feel.

Reinvent yourself as many times as you like

When you're still trying to determine who you are, you might present versions of yourself that don't truly reflect you. It's all part of figuring 'you' out. Even when you have figured you out, some versions of you will still be seasonal. Don't be afraid to reinvent yourself – or simply change your mind.

When I was a child, I thought all adults had their life figured out. Now I'm an adult, I realise that's just not the case. Everyday we're growing, developing, adapting and learning something new. I've also realised you can still be figuring things out and be happy.

I have reinvented myself more times than I can count. There was 'skater-girl Toni', who mimed to Avril Lavigne and wore XXL flares; there was 'pick-me Toni', who did the most to be liked by the guy she fancied; there was 'rebellious Toni', who lasted about ten working days, and the list goes on … Every time I would end one phase and start a new one, I'd feel a little bit guilty and ashamed. Guilty due to believing that I was a complete fraud, and ashamed for feeling like I had no real sense of identity. For whatever reason, it seemed as if everyone around me knew who they were and stood in their identities long term, but I just didn't feel like I knew myself. Who am I? What do I like? What do I dislike? Which group do I belong in? What makes me, me? These answers were forever changing, and at the time I hated it.

It wasn't until I grew a little older that I began to see the benefit of feeling 'lost'. In the moment it's a horrible feeling. My limited sense of identity felt crippling at times, but it also encouraged me to try new things, and in trying (whether you succeed or fail), you learn more about yourself. My skater-girl phase taught me that I hate skateboarding and that XXL flares definitely don't complement me; my pick-me phase taught me that the right guy will like you for you and pandering to the patriarchy is actually unhelpful, and my rebellious phase taught me that I'm not a rebel, and I find the presence of structure and rules somewhat calming. In every reinvention, I learned more about myself, and that learning brought me even closer to figuring out 'me'. Soon enough, I stopped seeing reinvention as something to be ashamed of. I started to view it as a fun part of my evolution. Change was no longer a sign of weakness to me, but a sign of strength. Once upon a time, the words 'you've changed' would send shivers down my spine, but the fact is, 'you've changed' is only a problem if you've changed for the worse. Society often paints change as if it's indicative of something negative – like an inability to remain consistent. But is consistency always a good thing? In my opinion, change as a form of evolution is wonderful, because nobody should stay exactly the same forever. If you're not evolving or growing, what are you doing? Embrace personal change if it means the you of today is better than the you of yesterday.

Do I feel like I'm still reinventing myself today? To a degree. I still take on new challenges and new hobbies, and I remind myself that I am never too old for a fresh start if I want one. We do ourselves a disservice when we tell ourselves we are too mature or too far gone for fresh starts. People start again all the time. If something isn't good for you, it's better to change it later than never at all – and if you want to reinvent yourself, you are well within your rights to, no matter what your age.

I think it's important that we give people the grace to grow and learn. It's also important that we give ourselves the same grace. Sometimes we say things that we believe in the moment, but with time new experiences can prompt our viewpoint to change. Sometimes we take on roles or opportunities we think we want, but with time we realise that we want something completely different. Other times we may invest in friendships or romantic relationships that make sense in the moment, but with time we recognise that they're not good for us. We have all had a change in opinion or perspective at some point in our life – we're human after all – so give yourself grace when you decide that it's time for a new beginning, a different road or a reinvention.

A stranger's opinion shouldn't matter more than yours

> *Caring about what other people think is normal. Just make sure your opinion of yourself holds the most weight.*

'I don't care what people think.' I'm sure you've heard someone say that before, or perhaps you've said it yourself. I used to be someone who said that sentence frequently, and I believed it too. I was so sure that I didn't care about what other people thought of me. I had always been very strong-willed and arguably stubborn, so I attributed my 'not caring' to this. It wasn't until my thirties that I re-evaluated the concept of not caring about what people think in a very simple and logical way. I asked myself some very basic questions: 'Do I want to be viewed as a bad person?' – the answer was no. 'Do I want to be viewed as friendly and kind?' – the answer was yes. In that moment I realised something blatantly obvious. On a basic and fundamental level, I *did* care about what people thought of me. I didn't want the general assessment of my character to be a bad one. I didn't want people to categorise me as an awful and unpleasant person. I didn't want my contribution to society to be viewed as negative. So, I cared. Did I care about the opinions of *specific* strangers? Not so much ... But when one opinion was part of a large collection of opinions, I cared. I cared about the very basic opinions people, and society as a collective, held about me. And the simple reality is that most of us do – whether we want to admit it or not.

If it's perfectly normal to care what people think, why then is there so much rhetoric surrounding *not* caring? I concluded that caring isn't the problem. The problem is caring about other people's opinion of you more than your own opinion of you. In all my musings about what I would do if the world saw me badly, one thing stood out more than anything else. What about me? What about the way *I* view myself? And what about the opinions of those dearest to me – the people who know me inside and out? Is it possible to care *too much* about what other people think?

What happens when we care too much about the thoughts and opinions of others?

We can end up living a life that is controlled purely by how people view us, instead of guided by what we want to get out of our own life.

Have you ever pursued something, or maybe even someone, purely because you're trying to impress others and not because you *genuinely* want it? At the end of the day, even if you succeed in this kind of pursuit, you never actually feel truly fulfilled and happy. The recognition and accolades you receive from others may satisfy you in the short term, but if that's not what you truly want for yourself, you'll feel like you sacrificed a part of your life for acceptance.

We could be led by others to the point where we succumb to peer pressure.

In some circumstances, peer pressure can be a very dangerous thing. Pressure from our peers could encourage us to do things we are uncomfortable with or even things that do not align with our values or our character. In fact, peer pressure and a desire to be liked and/or 'accepted' has led to some people doing things that have cost them their freedom or even their life.

We could put ourselves last.

When we care *too* much about what others think, we may also bend our backs and over-prioritise other people to our personal detriment. A strong desire to be liked is a very easy route to people-pleasing – which can encourage us to dismiss our own goals, needs or wants.

We don't implement boundaries.

Caring too much about other people's opinions may also prevent us from implementing boundaries, for fear of upsetting people or ruffling feathers. When we care too much about other people's opinions, we may end up protecting ourselves less, for the sake of keeping the peace or even aligning with the status quo.

If you recognise your habits in this chapter, you may be thinking about ways you can care less about the opinions of others. One way to start is to stop judging others. People who are prone to judging others tend to see the world in a very black-and-white way, and in turn they are under the impression that people judge them for the same reasons. When you incorporate more understanding, more compassion and less judgement in your day-to-day, you realise that everyone is entitled to live their life how they see fit. When you care less about how people choose to live their own lives, you begin to care less about how people may view yours.

Another way to care less about what others think is to take charge of your life, stand by your decisions and respect your own opinions. When we are constantly relying on people to validate our choices, we are suggesting that their opinion of our decisions holds more weight than our own. On your journey to not caring about what other people think, prioritise *your* choices and have faith in *your* decisions. Understand that nobody knows you better than you know yourself, and use that fact to strengthen your self-trust.

Comparing yourself to others less, and acknowledging the fact that nobody is perfect, is another way to care less about the opinions of others. Everyone is living their own life, with their own unique set of challenges. Who's to say that any single person's opinion of you holds more weight than your opinion – or any weight at all?

Working on developing self-love is also key to not caring so much about what people think. Caring about other people's opinions in such an intense way can be the result of us feeling unworthy and inadequate. Keeping company with people who uplift you, tracking your achievements, investing in yourself and doing the things you enjoy can give you the confidence boost you need to stand in your truth and prioritise your own opinion of yourself.

Lastly, stop centring yourself. The brutal but helpful truth is that the majority of the population don't care about what you're doing, because they're busy enough with what *they're* doing. Many times, we may think people care about our individual lives in a way that we should be concerned about – but the majority don't. And that's a good thing!

Overthinking is the enemy of happiness

> *Overthinking often does more harm than good. It exaggerates problems, it fabricates dilemmas, it encourages doubt, it feeds anxiety, it caters to pessimism … When you catch yourself overthinking, tell yourself you deserve to be happy and focus on something that facilitates this.*

My name is Toni, and I am a recovering overthinker. Overthinking is something that I have tackled my whole life. In some weird ways it has helped me (specifically when it comes to my writing), but in plenty of other ways, it has hurt me. Let me explain how bad it can get on its worst days … I can play an entire hypothetical scenario in my head from start to finish about something that likely won't even happen to me, but I can think about it enough that it negatively alters my mood. If that's not a sign of problematic overthinking, I don't know what is.

I've witnessed first-hand how overthinking can impact my life, and how it has impacted the lives of fellow overthinkers. For this reason, I believe that anyone who is prone to overthinking needs to try their best not to jeopardise the relationships in their life – whether that's friendships, business relationships, romantic relationships or family relationships. Below is a list of some of the things I've personally done to help me manage my mind:

1. Write down your thoughts
Keeping a journal or finding other outlets to express yourself that allow you to vent or manage your inner thoughts can help minimise overthinking. In my case, I took to social media to share my inner musings, which formed the foundation for my books. This is also evidence that, when channelled healthily, overthinking can be a source of creative inspiration.

2. Focus on solutions over the problems
When you focus solely on the 'problem', it's easy for it to grow or shapeshift in your mind. When you focus on how to resolve or 'fix' it, you're more likely to interpret the problem at hand as what it truly is. Also, being able

to see a light at the end of the tunnel helps to reduce anxiety, which in turn decreases your rate of overthinking.

3. Create new habits

One way you can create new and helpful habits is by constantly challenging your thoughts. Each time you consider what could go wrong in a scenario, follow up by asking yourself what could go right. Each time you worry about something out of your control, ask yourself what's in your control. Every time you think about a potential negative narrative, consider an alternative positive one. The more you do these things, the more instinctive they will become, and that's how you will end up creating new habits.

4. Keep track of the good things

Encouraging yourself to review the positives is another way to help yourself as an overthinker. Keep lists of the good things, save photos linked to great memories, store records of great experiences … When you find yourself overthinking about something small, reviewing these lists or memories can help shift your mood.

Overthinkers have an important role to play in not sabotaging certain aspects of their life. But that said, if you have an overthinker in your life that you care about, there are also things you can do to help your communication with them.

1. Be honest and transparent

You may think withholding or twisting the truth will prevent the overthinker in your life from overthinking, but it does more harm than good. If they discover the truth or sense you're withholding things, it will just make their overthinking ten times worse. Be as transparent as you can be and try your very best not to unsettle them in ways that can make them spiral.

2. Consider how you share information

You also need to consider how you relay things to an overthinker – particularly because they pay an immense level of attention to body language and words. It's not that they require constant reassurance, they just want to feel like you mean what you say and say what you mean.

3. Be intentional

Overthinkers are also very big on the 'why' of things. Why did they do this? Why did they say this? Why did they withhold this? Your intentions matter greatly to them, because without you even knowing, they are pondering your intent all the time. That's why, when you're with an overthinker, it's good to ask yourself about your own intentions when you're communicating certain things to them. Why are you sharing what you're sharing, and how can you share it in a way that will comfort them and/or won't alarm them?

4. Say what you mean

Understanding the power of words and being able to control your words is also very important. Don't say things you don't mean. Also, as crucial as words are, actions are just as important. Like with any relationship, make sure your actions mirror the things you say.

5. Be patient

Managing your frustrations is also key when you have an overthinker in your life, because overthinkers like detail, and as a result they may ask you plenty of questions – sometimes about things you may consider insignificant. They may even bring up a topic from the past for further clarity.

Life as an overthinker, or friendships and other relation-ships with an overthinker, require an added level of effort. However, when both people understand that they have to meet one another in the middle, it can help transform what could have been an anxious life and connection into a peaceful and fulfilling one.

How you speak to yourself, and about yourself, has a direct impact on your life

There is one opinion you will hear more than any other – and that is your opinion of yourself. You cannot escape your thoughts, or that voice in your head, so the best thing you can do for you is to make that voice a kind one.

One of the most helpful skills I now possess is my ability to speak to myself with compassion. I'm a natural optimist (which helps), but sometimes, even for the most positive of us, speaking to yourself with kindness can prove to be a challenge. It's not uncommon for people to be much harder on themselves than they are on others. After all, we know so much about ourselves. We know our own thoughts, drivers and desires, so judging ourselves more harshly is a very easy thing to do.

It can also be a dangerous thing to do. While the ability to self-reflect and hold yourself accountable is important, it's equally important for people to monitor *how* they do this. When it's done uncompassionately, it can quite easily turn into negative self-talk.

Ways to tell the difference between normal healthy inner dialogue and negative self-talk:

Negative self-talk is limiting. It doesn't encourage us to keep going in order to deliver better results. Instead, it encourages us to give up completely.

Have you ever embarked on something (whether it's a job, hobby or relationship) and made a mistake in the process? Perhaps you thought you failed at it in some way. When we negatively self-talk, we tell ourselves to stop what we're doing entirely and perhaps never do it again. For example: 'I suck at this. I'm never going to get it right. I should just give up. Clearly this isn't for me.' When we talk to ourselves with compassion, we can acknowledge that we may not be the best at something now, but we understand that with time and practice we can get better.

Negative self-talk is unforgiving. It leaves little to no room for mistakes.

Human beings are imperfect, and as a result we often make mistakes in life. Sometimes they're small, other times they're large, but whatever the mistake, they're ours to own and learn from. When we negatively self-talk, we are typically very unforgiving when we make mistakes. We are hard on ourselves in a way that implies perfection is the only option. Forgiving yourself is important, and real forgiveness isn't about ignoring the mistake – it's about acknowledging it, holding yourself accountable, but also reminding yourself that although you may not be able to change the past, you have an opportunity to change your outcomes and choices in the future.

Negative self-talk is belittling. It focuses on weaknesses and inabilities, and internalises them.

People who often engage in negative self-talk typically include quite negative adjectives in their regular vocabulary. 'Stupid', 'ugly', 'failure' and 'useless' are words they would often use to describe themselves. Words like this shouldn't exist in your descriptions of yourself because negative self-talk is rarely constructive. It rarely leads to positive change. It just leads to diminished self-esteem. Instead, acknowledge your weaknesses or inabilities in ways that help you grow. For example, you could turn 'I'm so stupid for messing this up' into 'I didn't do it correctly this time, but now I've learned how not to do it, I'll do it even better in the future.'

Negative self-talk is quick to envy rather than admire. It is also quick to compare rather than learn.

Compassionate self-talkers do a good job of being easy on themselves when presented with other people's happiness and successes. When someone is a negative self-talker, it's not uncommon for them to say things like: 'Why is my business not doing as well as theirs? I hate how happy they are. It's so unfair.' Negative self-talkers will often compare their life to other people's in ways that make them feel bad about the life they have. A compassionate self-talker may still compare, but in a way that is motivating, with a view to learning and not putting themselves down. So instead of seeing other people's successes as an unfair advantage or something to hate, they may say: 'Wow, they look so happy. I can't wait for my business to succeed! I wonder what they did that I could maybe learn from.'

You might be thinking, 'This is great and all, but it's way easier said than done.' This is true. Mastering your inner voice is no easy task, but it's something you can improve with practice. You need to be your own accountability captain. Remind yourself that if you wouldn't talk to the people you love in that way, you shouldn't talk to yourself in that way either. And in the moments when you catch yourself talking to yourself uncompassionately, check yourself and, in your head (or out loud if you're comfortable), say, 'I deserve to talk to myself with love.'

We owe it to ourselves to train our inner voice to be kind to us.

Ask for help when you need it

Some people aren't good at asking for help because they're so used to being 'the helper'. Throughout their life they've experienced an unbalanced give and take, so their instinct is usually 'I'll figure it out on my own'. Self-reliance is all they've ever known.

Last year, my best friend reached out to me to stress that she was there for me should I ever need to talk. She said what she said because I'm so terrible at seeking support or advice from people. As the eldest of three children (the first daughter of an immigrant family at that), I have done a lot of 'leading' in my life. I grew up with a debilitating sense of 'duty'. I felt as if it was my duty to 'keep it together' and 'be strong' for the sake of my family. I felt as if it was my duty to give more than I got. I felt as if it was my duty to centre and prioritise the needs of other people before my own. I'm the person people go to for help, not the other way around. And as such, I have a reputation for being hyper-resilient, but that's not necessarily a good thing. I do a lot for myself and by myself because I can hold myself accountable, I know exactly what I'm thinking, and I deem myself reliable and trustworthy. In my mind, I can handle the pressure, I'll figure it out (because I always do), and nobody will do a better job than me. But I also do a lot for myself out of fear. Fear of relying on people, fear of being disappointed, fear of not being taken seriously should I ask for help, fear of appearing incompetent for requiring support and fear of regret. Before even attempting to ask for help, I would tell myself things like, 'Nobody cares about my problems,' or, 'Everyone thinks I don't need help, so why would they give it to me?' Much of my self-sufficiency was heightened by fear, as well as being a side effect of bearing the brunt of responsibility as the oldest in my family.

I spent so much of my adolescence and young adult life being self-reliant in my own way that I just couldn't fathom the thought of seeking out assistance. It wasn't until one day, in my late twenties, that I had a total meltdown. I was in my family home, with my siblings and parents, and was completely overwhelmed that day. Before I knew it, I couldn't hold the tears in and I broke down about feeling underappreciated. At the time I felt like my loved ones expected and got so much from me, while I expected and got so much less from them. It wasn't until my sister said: 'But, Toni, when do you ever ask for help?' In that instant I realised that what I viewed as an unbalanced give-and-take was somewhat fed by my unwillingness to speak up about how I was feeling and my reflex to get everything done on my own. Now, one might argue that I shouldn't have to speak up and people should consider how I'm coping when it comes to all that I do, but the truth is that people are not mind readers. While it's considerate to take time out to check on others, not doing so doesn't automatically make someone uncaring or malicious. Everyone is going through their own set of challenges, and sometimes their lack of checking in is purely a result of just being so busy with their own day-to-day. The care they have isn't only displayed by proactively checking in. It can also be displayed in how they react when you speak up. So I began to do exactly that. I began to speak up – to challenge the imbalance that I had enabled.

Not sure how you can get better at asking for help? For me, the first step towards battling my reluctance was considering the benefits. 'How will their support benefit me and my situation?' Understanding the benefits helps us to validate the importance of asking. Another tip involves reminding yourself that everyone needs help at some point. Requesting help or support during challenging times is absolutely normal and does not make you weak. Also, communicate using methods that make you feel most comfortable. For example, it's much easier for me to ask for help over the phone than in person. For you, it may be easier over text message than in a call. Do what makes you feel most comfortable to ease yourself in. In addition, be discerning about who you ask. Unfortunately, it's not everybody you can comfortably ask for help. Some people are much better candidates than others. Consider the kind of support you need, your relationship with the other person and their weaknesses/strengths. That should help you determine who to go to. Lastly, be mindful of the language you use. One thing I dislike when people ask me for help is if they do so with entitlement – no 'please', no 'thank you', no checking if I'm available to support; just an expectation that I will deliver. While you may hope that the person you ask is able to help you, be careful not to sound demanding – ask how you would like to be asked.

Generally, the worst that can happen when we ask for support is that we are not given it. In those moments, remind yourself that there will always be other people or resources you can go to. Also, don't let a 'no' impact how you view asking. Sometimes we will sadly face rejection before we get the support we truly want, but rejection shouldn't prevent you from continuing to search.

Hyper-independence can be debilitating. On the one hand it's a strength, because it helps you get things done. But it can also be a weakness because there is power in community and support systems. As independent as I am, I acknowledge that when I am surrounded by people who care for me, I am greater as part of a team. There is strength in asking for help, and as the popular African proverb suggests, 'If you want to go fast, go alone. If you want to go far, go together.'

Your twenties are your first decade of adulthood

The moment a person reaches their twenties, society puts so much pressure on them to have everything in order, while forgetting that they have never 'adulted' before. Your twenties provide a unique opportunity to learn, re-learn, grow, adapt, develop and change. You're not meant to have everything figured out. You're meant to discover what being an adult means to you.

When I was a child, I remember thinking twenty-something was so grown up. In my mind, being in your twenties was the pinnacle of adulthood and anything after that was pretty much elderly. After all, my favourite celebrities as a child were in their twenties, so that had to be your prime, *right?* When I was a teen, I was so sure that by the age of 25 I'd have a house, a husband, a dog and a million sitting in my bank account. Boy, was I wrong! It wasn't until I reached my twenties that I realised twenty-something wasn't actually that grown up at all. Did I feel like I had a greater sense of freedom once I became an adult? Yes, I did. But in a weird way, I also felt like a child. I still felt young and unready, but with more responsibilities – and there was no formal schooling for adulthood. It was literally a case of 'learn as you go'.

So I proceeded to learn as I went. The journey to learning was certainly not a simple one. By the time 25 came, I felt like if life was a game, I was losing. As far as I was concerned, I was behind … and I was failing. This led me to compare my circumstances with other people's, but I rarely felt better for it and often felt worse. I was desperate to achieve *something* in my mid-twenties, but I just didn't know what that something was.

Once 25, 26 and 27 came and went, I attempted to unlearn what being twenty-something was all about. I felt dissatisfied with my life, and as long as I told myself my age had to define my achievements, I knew I would never be at peace. I did a lot of soul searching – which involved considering where the ridiculous idea that you had to have everything sorted by twenty-something came from. I concluded that I – and many other twenty-somethings — were victims of history. We were victims of societal standards that were set at a different time, when people had different expectations. When our grandparents were growing up, it was normal to be married and have children by the age of 30. Your twenties were your defining years, the years of massive change — and people were encouraged to grow up 'quickly'. I reflected on the fact that different eras produce different results. People may have been buying homes and settling down in their twenties in 1950, but with the evolution of human rights (particularly women's rights), and the rising costs of living, why was I ascribing outdated expectations to my life? In fact, why was I trying to align with any expectations? Was it because I truly desired a husband, a house and a picket fence in my twenties or because I cared too much about what other people thought?

It eventually hit me. My twenties weren't about being financially free, getting married, comparing myself to my peers or feeling as if I should have all the wisdom in the world. They were about enjoying my first adult decade and not being hard on myself while I discovered who I was. My childhood twenties 'to-do list' wasn't achieved, and I still don't have some of those things, but looking back, I'm not mad about it.

Twenty-somethings: don't be so hard on yourself. Success and love can come at any time. Your twenties are your first decade of adulthood, so experience new things, explore the world, grow, learn. Stop putting a deadline on your timeline. Life is a journey, not a race.

Things don't always happen according to your deadlines

Have you ever felt like something is meant for you, but it just isn't your time yet? Like you know deep down it's going to happen for you, but you also know something else is meant to happen first. And that thing that has to happen first will make what is meant for you ten times better.

In today's world, it's very easy to compare yourself to others, particularly because opportunity for comparison is everywhere (thanks, social media). As a result, you can end up living your life according to the timelines presented to you by society, instead of the timeline that is best for you.

Things don't always happen for you when you want them to. People often focus on the blessings they want to receive, without considering whether they're actually ready to receive them. Sometimes the delay in receiving your blessing isn't a result of it not being meant for you. It may be meant for you, but just not right now.

Outside of going to university, the first time I lived in my own place was when I was 31 years old. Until the age of 31, I lived in my family home, with my parents. I recall numerous occasions in person and online that involved people querying why I was living at home – in a tone that was always more belittling than curious. 'Aren't you a little too old to be living with your parents?' 'Are you embarrassed by the fact that you still live at home?' 'So how the hell does living with your parents at your age actually work?' 'You still live with your parents at your big age?' It was as if my choices and my timeline irritated people. After all, according to Western society, I should be out of my family home and renting my own place by 21, right?

Wrong. By the age of 21, I should have been 21 – but people around me felt the need to impose their own timelines and pressures on my life, as if aligning with these things meant I was more valuable to society – and them. Thankfully, I did what worked for me. I remained at home long enough to save money and feel comfortable with the prospect of moving to a different city. What many people also fail to realise is that having the ability and choice to stay in your family home – for as long as you require – is actually a privilege. It's a luxury that is sadly not accessible to everyone. Some people don't have positive relationships with their family members, and for that reason they're unable to live comfortably at home. Others are kicked out, against their preference. Some may not even have a place to call 'home'. It's an unfortunate reality, yet many people don't consider staying at home to be a benefit – but rather a privilege to be ashamed of. This is also a very Western approach. In many cultures, it is perfectly acceptable and common for grown-up children to remain at home until they get married or can afford their own place, and that was the view my parents took – so I made the choice to stay, and I'm very thankful for it, because it really paid off. My first out-of-home experience was a two-bed luxury apartment, with an en-suite master bedroom, secure underground parking and amenities, which included a gym and private cinema room. Many of the same people who queried my being at home also gushed about how nice my apartment was – and I found it very ironic. It was ironic because me choosing to stay at home for as long as I did put me in the perfect position to find my first apartment during the perfect window of time – when I could afford it.

A lot of things I wanted for myself five years ago I now have. I remember feeling frustrated about so many aspects of my life, often wondering when it would be 'my time'. I was in a job that I wasn't passionate about and had no sense of purpose for myself. I was in a relationship that seemed to be going nowhere slowly. And I was in debt and had no idea how I would get out of it. As far as I was concerned, there was so much in my life that was going wrong, and all I wanted was for things to change.

Things obviously did change, but they didn't change immediately or according to my timeline – or the timeline other people wanted to project onto me. It took a couple of years for everything to fall into place. In hindsight, I wasn't ready to receive a lot of the things I wanted for myself. For example, my desire to be in a relationship that progressed to marriage quickly wasn't due to me feeling like I had met someone who had all the qualities I wanted in a partner. Nor was it due to me being ready to build a partnership and enter a lifetime commitment. It was because, in my mind, marriage was the next thing on my life 'to-do list', and the idea of it made sense to me, considering I had been in that relationship for three years at the time.

Another thing I wasn't ready for was my dream job. I'm doing this job now, but I got here after recognising that achieving what I wanted to achieve required work. I wanted marriage for the wrong reasons, and I wanted my dream job without putting any real work in. If I'd had the job I now have five years ago, I wouldn't have appreciated it in the same way and would have likely made a mess of any opportunities I was presented with.

Similarly, when it came to my debt, in hindsight it was something I had to experience to improve my understanding of finances and my relationship with money. I can't speak for everyone else, but if I had come into contact with the kind of money I have access to now, I would have most certainly remained in debt, or even worse – increased the debt I was in. Having money requires a responsible mindset, and five years ago I definitely wasn't as responsible with money as I am now. It was something I was forced to learn.

All these examples just go to show that blessings aren't always delivered when we want them. Sometimes they come when we're actually truly ready to receive them. In my mid-twenties, I wasn't in alignment to receive, appreciate and make the most of the blessings I was hoping for. In the moment I didn't realise that, though … It wasn't until I really started to put in that self-work that things started to fall into place.

You may be feeling as if you're not doing something 'on time'. Perhaps it's also moving out of your family home, or maybe it's getting married, or getting a salaried job, or having children. Whatever it is, you cannot put a deadline on your timeline. I know I've written this already, but I will continue to stress this until it sinks in. In my case, everything happened when it was supposed to happen. I discovered that my time was my time, and I tried my best not to allow external ridicule or questions to get to me. It's not an easy thing to do, especially when people make you feel bad for moving at your own pace, but the thing is, that's exactly what it is – your own pace. Not theirs, or someone else's, but yours.

I don't know what it is about the world we live in, but people often want to replicate everyone else's journey. If enough people are doing something around the same time, then suddenly that becomes 'the rule' for everybody, and I hate it. I don't think people should get married in their twenties; I think people should get married if or when they meet someone they want to marry. I don't think people should move out when they're 21; I think people should move out when their circumstances are aligned with moving out and it's in their best interests.

Your job isn't to replicate someone else's success or life. Your job is to carve out what success means to you, and to enjoy your life on your own terms. Instead of mimicking someone else's story, write your own.

Nobody knows when you're supposed to do anything and why – not even you. And as scary as it is sometimes, there's also a beauty in not knowing how your life will turn out. When there's mystery, there's room for change, and you should appreciate that freedom. If things aren't happening for you now, don't lose hope. Your life can change significantly in a short space of time. You never know what's around the corner. Learn from your mistakes, invest in yourself, don't be too self-critical and embrace progress over perfection.

Find joy in ageing

> *One thing that keeps me going is believing that the best years of my life are still ahead of me. Ageing is inevitable, so why not learn to embrace it in a way that suits you? If you see it as an issue, you're guaranteeing negative emotions with every year that passes. Find joy in appreciating the fact that you're still here.*

One thing I've never really had an issue with is ageing in a biological sense. While I felt pressure in my twenties to achieve certain things by a certain age, the thought of getting older in general wasn't one that scared me. I think I can thank my mother for this. My mother is someone who never really referenced her age as a negative thing. If anything, she treated ageing like a blessing – which it undeniably is, because the opposite of ageing is ... well ... not ageing, and if you're not ageing, that means you're not living. And who wants that?

In my late twenties, I was surprised to discover that my attitude to ageing wasn't as common as I thought it was. For the first time in my life, my peers began freaking out about their age – more specifically, turning 30. I'm giggling as I write this because 30 is still very young, but on a more serious note, women in particular have been led to believe their twenties are their 'prime' years and that anything after 29 is out of style and geriatric. Once my peers and I finally hit 30, that's when I suddenly began to notice the age-shaming online – most commonly from young women.

Age shaming is one thing I will never understand. As if everyone doesn't age! Women age-shaming other women is even more nonsensical to me. It only reinforces patriarchy. When you shame other women for being older than you, you're suggesting that women lose their value beyond a certain age, and that our value is tied only to our youth and physical appearance. So what happens to the shamer once they age? Does this mean they too will be worthless according to their own standards? The same grace we give to men regarding ageing should be given to women. In my opinion, so many women become even more beautiful as they get older. It's in their wisdom, their intelligence, their grace, their experience … A superficial person cannot see the benefits of ageing, but a person with substance definitely can.

When people age-shame online, the petty part of me really wants to say, 'May you never age' – but as I stated previously, the opposite of ageing is not living and I don't want to wish death on anybody, no matter how nasty their comments might be.

The simple fact about ageing is that, with every year you live, you have gained a year of experience, a year of wisdom, a year of understanding yourself even better. Might you face certain challenges that come with being older? Yes. But getting older means you've been blessed with another year of life, and being alive is the biggest blessing that has been bestowed on all of us.

Develop a gratitude habit

Sometimes the only thing standing in between us and a better mood is an expression of gratitude. Make a habit of expressing gratitude regularly. It's much easier to feel happier when you realise you have things to be thankful for.

One thing I've always tried to do as part of my daily routine is express gratitude. In a world where people are often so preoccupied with wanting more, it can be very easy to feel dissatisfied with your life – constantly chasing things, because what you have never seems to be enough.

I think it's important for us to strive to be the best version of ourselves, and to attempt to reach our fullest potential, but a desire for more doesn't have to come with discontentment and dissatisfaction. Through all my ambitions and goals for myself, I try my very best to remind myself that gratitude and ambition can co-exist. Will I stop working on myself? No. Will I continue to strive for a better life (in terms of what 'better' means to me)? Yes. Does this mean I must be ungrateful about the life I currently have? Far from it.

The effectiveness of showing regular gratitude has been proven in several studies. One such study was in 2003, entitled 'Counting blessings versus burdens: an experimental investigation of gratitude and subjective well-being in daily life'.* Carried out by Dr Robert Emmons and Dr Michael McCullough, the study involved a number of participants being asked to keep a record each week of three specific topics. The first group of participants wrote about things that annoyed or irritated them, the second about things that had affected them in general, and the third group wrote about things they were grateful for. After a number of weeks, the gratitude group expressed better life satisfaction and fewer hospital visits – which is unsurprising as other research suggests people who regularly express gratitude have lower blood pressure and better immune systems. Additional studies have further supported the notion that keeping a record of things

---

* Robert A Emmons, Michael E McCullough, 'Counting blessings versus burdens: an experimental investigation of gratitude and subjective well-being in daily life', February 2003.

you're grateful for improves a person's level of happiness in general.

So how does one get started if they've never really made a habit of expressing gratitude before? One way is to keep a gratitude diary. Each evening, write about something you were grateful for that day. It could be something big or small – it doesn't matter. Just reflect on why you appreciated it. Another way to show gratitude is to thank people. Thank-you notes, thank-you cards or simply just communicating in person all help to remind us that there are people in our lives who are making a positive and helpful impact. Lastly, if you're religious you can pray, and if you're not religious you can meditate. Taking five minutes out of your day to communicate/think about all the things you're thankful for is another simple way to incorporate an expression of gratitude into your daily routine.

The life you are currently living is the foundation for tomorrow – the bricks you're laying for your future. There is no better tomorrow without a today. In recognition of this, remain thankful for your health, your experiences, your loved ones, their health and the opportunities you have been presented with that can help you build an even better future for yourself.

You can be 'nice' without dismissing your wants and needs

> *Being too polite or too 'nice' because you don't want to hurt people's feelings will have you saying you like your hair in the salon, then crying on your way home. I've learned that life is too short to disregard your own preferences. It's important to know when to speak up if you dislike things.*

I used to think it was impossible to be 'too nice'. Surely being a polite, kind and compassionate human being can only be a good thing? The reality is that too much of anything can be an issue. Sometimes people can equate niceness with being agreeable – but agreeable to their own detriment. For example, some people are so desperate to be viewed as nice that they struggle to voice their needs – which includes their likes and dislikes. I used to be one of these people. For the longest time I would swallow my feelings for the sake of not hurting other people's feelings, for the sake of not wanting to seem like a problem or simply because I was too scared to assert my wants. I used to keep quiet to keep the peace, but that's because I was more focused on maintaining everyone else's peace than I was on ensuring my own. Every time I swallowed my feelings, only one person felt the brunt of it – and that person was me. Why was I so wrapped up in preserving other people's opinions of me or their own feelings at the expense of my own?

If you're an empath, you're naturally in tune with other people's emotions, but feeling overly responsible for the feelings of others can have a significant impact on the way you feel. And the way you feel is important. The way you feel matters. Recognising this can be the difference between living a happy life and an unhappy one. This doesn't mean you should live your life selfishly, dismissing the feelings of everyone and anyone around you. It just means that, while you regard the feelings of others, you do not disregard your own.

Signs that you may be 'too nice' include:

- Feeling the urge to say 'sorry' when you're not even in the wrong.
- Constantly apologising for other people's mistakes.

- Regularly invalidating your own feelings and needs to make other people happy or comfortable.
- Agreeing with people even when you don't, in order to be compliant.
- Deprioritising your needs and putting other people first in a way that jeopardises your own happiness.
- Rarely saying 'no'.

One lesson I learned in my twenties is that some people think they're nice, but really they just struggle to implement boundaries. Their niceness isn't always led by compassion and care – sometimes it's led by insecurity and fear. It's intimidation and anxiousness disguised as niceness.

Frankly, being nice doesn't have to mean being agreeable. Being nice doesn't mean you have to put yourself last either. For me, niceness is about consideration, honesty and kind communication.

How to be nice without hurting yourself:

- You consider the impact on others in the things you do and the decisions you make – but know that this doesn't mean you have to do what they want all the time.
- You are honest with yourself and those around you about how you feel, because holding in resentment, annoyance and anger will only fuel negativity in you.
- You communicate your honest feelings as kindly as you can, because lying to yourself and others is not a healthy habit, and you are kind in how you communicate and talk about others in general.

So next time you want to dismiss your needs and wants because you think it's the nice thing to do, please don't. By all means consider other people, but also consider yourself, always.

You're allowed to change your mind

> *Don't stick with decisions you no longer align with out of fear of disappointing people. You're allowed to change your mind. Take control of your life. If you no longer want or like something, communicate that. Just do it with grace and compassion.*

One part of life that is important to consider is the way your beliefs, choices and decisions can change. This is an inevitable aspect of self-reinvention and evolution, but outside of the more elaborate forms of change, your mind can change in general over the course of a few hours, minutes or even seconds. There's a lot of emphasis placed on sticking to your guns, but while standing firm in certain decisions can be helpful, it can also be very unhelpful – and people who change their mind tend to have very valid reasons for doing so.

Valid reasons for changing your mind include:

- Your initial choice reflected what someone else wanted for you, not what you truly want for yourself.
- Something traumatic has happened, which makes you feel unsafe or worried about your initial choice.
- Something amazing has happened, which makes you feel like you're going to make a better choice the second time around.
- You were pressured and/or made your initial choice in haste without accurately assessing the situation.
- You have been presented with new information that changes how you view your initial choice.
- Your preferences have changed in line with your progression.
- Because you can.

Being able to change your mind and make snap decisions is arguably a survival technique. If new information or circumstances are presented to you, your willingness to change your mind could be the difference between life or death (okay, I know this is rather dramatic, but it's true). In addition, changing your mind allows you to review situations from a range of perspectives. With every new decision, you connect to new justifications, and every new justification brings a new level of understanding. One could easily infer that people who are open to changing their mind are less judgemental, more compassionate and more tolerant.

The thing is, your mind is yours to change as you see fit. It's not something you should approach with remorse or embarrassment. It's a normal part of growth. The person we were yesterday isn't the same as the person we are today, and therefore the things we wanted yesterday aren't always the same things we want today.

Everyone is not you

> *Everyone is not you. People are motivated by different things, they dislike different things, they prioritise different things; they love differently, they think differently, they live DIFFERENTLY. You can't change people. Just surround yourself with people you can gel with.*

One hard lesson I had to learn growing up was that everyone is not me. I can recall many moments in the past when I would show disdain at another person's choices, only to be confronted with 'Not everyone is like you, though' by a friend. I would often attempt to explain what I would have done in a situation, only to be told, 'Yeah, but not everyone thinks like you.' Or I'd even debate with another person about a decision they'd made or an action they had carried out, only to hear, 'But I'm not you.' Eventually, after hearing similar statements for long enough, you tend to get the point.

It's very easy to live in a projection – projecting your upbringing, values, lifestyle and motivations onto everyone else. Unfortunately, like many individuals, I assumed people saw life in the exact same way as me – through my own lens. I would find myself feeling so angry when someone would behave in a way that I didn't understand. I expected everyone else to mirror my energy, my effort, my understanding, my level of care, my enthusiasm – whether that was in the workplace, in friendships or other relationships.

Much harder than living in a projection is accepting a difference in reality. This involves stepping out of yourself and assessing the world in a way that makes room for individual differences and unique experiences. Putting yourself in another person's shoes is a lot more difficult than expecting the world to wear your own. With time, I came to the realisation that my analysis of the world around me was one based solely on my own personal experiences and thoughts. When you understand this, you come to the conclusion that people are rarely influenced by you and you alone.

Next time you find yourself feeling frustrated by other people's actions or decisions, tell yourself four very simple things:

- They did not grow up in your household.
- They have been through things you know nothing about.
- Everything they have experienced up to now has shaped them.
- They are who they are because they lived a totally different life to you.

These reminders helped me to show people grace and compassion. Admittedly, in my teen years and early twenties I was quite judgemental – largely because I saw the world through my lens alone, with no room for a change in perspective or a real effort at understanding. When I began reminding myself of the above points, my judgements reduced and my willingness to leave people to live their own lives increased. I learned that I cannot force people to do as I do, but I can try to understand why they might do things in a different way and, in turn, I shouldn't be so quick to judge people for this. So next time you find yourself being critical because some-one chooses to live differently to you, understand that nobody is born with innate wisdom. Their choices are a result of their experiences, and your choices are simply a result of yours.

'Nothing other people do is because of you. It is because of themselves. All people live in their own dream, in their own mind; they are in a completely different world from the one we live in. When we take something personally, we make the assumption that they know what is in our world, and we try to impose our world on their world.'

– Don Miguel Ruiz, *The Four Agreements: A Practical Guide to Personal Freedom*

Not every good thing is too good to be true

> *Is it too good to be true or are you too traumatised by the past to accept the present for what it is?*

Some people are scared of good things. If you're not like this, you might be thinking, 'Why would anyone be scared of something good?,' but it's a common trait, and one that I've seen in some of my own acquaintances, friends and family members.

From my personal observations, this fear of a good thing is often tied to a past experience or an absence of positivity in the past. For some people, their childhood was devoid of certain joys, so the feeling of being presented with something good is so foreign to them, and the thought of things working out is so strange, that when they are confronted with something good or great they panic. They talk themselves out of enjoying the process because they're too used to things not working in their favour. For other people, another aspect of their life was traumatising. Perhaps they went through a difficult friendship in the past, and for that reason any subsequent friendship (no matter how good) is picked apart and overanalysed. Or maybe they thought they got their dream job, which turned out to be a job from hell, so now they think every new opportunity they are offered is a trap.

When we've experienced a traumatic past event, it might be that we end up seeing genuinely good people, opportunities or jobs as too good to be true even when they're not. Sometimes the problem doesn't lie in the situation; it lies in our own projections. Does this mean nothing is ever too good to be true? Sadly, no. Sometimes we are presented with things that seem good on the surface, but that aren't good at all. Being able to discern whether there is an actual issue at hand or whether you are actively looking for problems is important.

So … how do you tell the difference? Well, there's no way to be 100-per-cent certain, but there are signs:

There is evidence to support why it is happening.

If someone knocked on my door today to offer me a large sum of money to cook a private dinner, I'd be anxious about it and inclined to question the legitimacy of the offer, because after all, I'm not a professional chef. If someone offered me a large sum of money to write another book – even if it was *extremely* large – I wouldn't be anxious, because writing is what I do for a living, and there is evidence to support why they have chosen me. If something enters your life based on evidence that is present, reflect on that evidence. Imposter syndrome often encourages us to invalidate our achievements and see opportunities as flukes or luck, but as lucky as we may all hope to be, good opportunities rarely arise because of pure luck alone. Something happened to generate the opportunity – so always consider the evidence.

There is no evidence to support that it may be bad. Typically, whenever I have encountered anything that is genuinely too good to be true, there have been flags to suggest this is the case. These flags were never internal feelings of anxiousness in isolation; rather, my internal feelings of anxiousness were triggered by the presence of these amber (or even red) flags. For example, when I have encountered potential opportunities but they require a payment from me before I can even access said opportunity (aka a scam), that's a flag. Alternatively, if

I'm developing a potential new relationship with someone who seems amazing but is very secretive about their past, that's a flag. If, on the other hand, there is absolutely no external negative evidence to suggest that what is being presented to me is bad, it just might be a good thing!

Simply put, stop talking yourself out of good things, and it's important that you stop labelling every good thing as 'too good to be true'. You are good enough to receive good things, and good things are meant to happen to you.

Section 2:
Friendships

Everyone needs a friend. Good friends enrich our lives. They increase our sense of belonging and community. They improve our self-confidence. They help us grow as people, they laugh with us, they make memories with us, they encourage us, they listen to us and they love us. Several studies even go so far as to state that having good friends makes us healthier people. One multigenerational Harvard study,* which ran from 1983 to 2003,

* James H Fowler, Nicholas A Christakis, 'Dynamic spread of happiness in a large social network: longitudinal analysis over 20 years in the Framingham Heart Study', February 2008.

also concluded that having happy friends makes us happier in turn.

So, what makes a good friend? In my opinion, a good friend has the following qualities:

- They are trustworthy and honest.
- They respect you and others.
- They speak kindly about you – even when you're not around.
- They give you room to be yourself.
- They want the best for you.
- They are happy to see you happy.
- They respect your boundaries.
- They uplift you and support you.
- They are dependable.
- They listen.

While I am a very family-orientated person and spend most of my time with my family members, I can't deny that my strongest friendships have added a lot of value to my life. Some of my fondest memories have been created with my closest friends, and some of my most valuable lessons have been generated by my interactions with them.

FRIENDSHIPS

In this section of my book, I want you to take note of the lessons I learned from gaining friends, losing friends and maintaining friendships.

Be mindful of the company you keep

> *The people you spend the most time with will rub off on you. Their behaviours, beliefs and words will contribute to the person you are becoming – whether you're aware of it or not. Be selective when it comes to the company you choose to keep.*

'Birds of a feather flock together' is a saying many of us have heard at some point. Do I agree with this statement? Yes and no. On the one hand, it is very possible to be quite different from our friends. For example, my best friend is a clear and obvious extrovert, and I am not. My best friend has different passions to me, a different love language to me, different strengths and different weaknesses. Although we are besties, we are two very different people in many ways. However, we are friends because of our similarities, whether that's our shared values, shared hobbies, shared personality traits or complementary communication styles. We are different birds, but also birds of a feather. So for this reason, I don't believe this saying suggests that we are just like our friends. I think it suggests that for a friendship to exist, there needs to be something shared, which connects you on some level – otherwise, why be friends in the first place?

When it comes to friendships, I am most certainly a 'quality over quantity' kind of person. According to British anthropologist, Robin Dunbar, while the average person has the capacity to maintain several connections at once, people typically have only five *very* close friends – with this inner circle typically including one or more family members.* Dunbar's theory is certainly true for me. I think it's important to cultivate a diverse network, but as far as the number of people that I'd share my deepest secrets with goes, I can count exactly five (which includes my family members). I'm all for friendships that occur organically. I can't force a friendship just to be part of a clique, or because someone is successful, or because people think I should hang out with a person. A genuine friendship must occur naturally. Friendships, for me, are about mutual trust, mutual care, mutual

* Robin Dunbar, 'Friends: Understanding the Power of Our Most Important Relationships', March 2021.

understanding, mutual respect and mutual interests. I would much rather (and do) have just a few friends that I can trust wholeheartedly than many friends who don't tick those boxes. Even when my friends and I demonstrate some differences, it's these mutual shared values that determine our friendship.

When we build new friendships, it's important for us to ask ourselves what makes us want to be friends with the person in the first place (and vice versa). What did you have in common that caused you to strike up your initial interaction? I say this because over the years, from being a teen until now, I have been repeatedly shocked at the fact that some people initiate friendships with others for what can be deemed as quite shallow and materialistic reasons. For example: 'You're pretty/popular/rich, I want to be your friend.' The problem with these types of friends is that they rarely care enough.

They tend to be people who like the 'idea' of you. They have a superficial vision of you in their head and that's what they are attracted to. Surface-level stuff. The moment they are no longer reaping the superficial benefits that come with being your friend, they retreat … because you no longer align with the vision they created, and they have less to gain from being connected to you.

I personally like being friends with people I don't have to second-guess. Those friends who don't make me worry about what they might say behind my back. Friends I can put my complete trust in. These are the people I have time for. The people I'm happy to call friends.

Does this mean all your friendships must be extremely deep and meaningful? Not at all. Different friends can add value in different places. It's okay to have different friends for different things. You might have one you party with, one you have vulnerable and deep conversations with, one you talk business with, one you travel with, etc. Sometimes they're all the same person, but even if they're not, that's okay … Your friendships don't have to be as meaningful as each other, but they shouldn't be built on factors that compromise your character or go against your values.

Why is this important? Our friends are an extension of us to some degree – whether we like it or not. They reflect the things we value, the things we hold dear, where we are in our lives, what we prioritise. Even when we have some differences with them, friends who align with our core values help us remain true to ourselves. Our friendships can rub off on us in many ways. Good friends can help us grow, and bad friends can cause us to regress. When you select friends, be mindful of this.

Surround yourself with people who make you feel valued. Surround yourself with people who tell you the truth because they want you to be better. Surround yourself with people who encourage you to love yourself. Surround yourself with people you can be your truest self around. You don't have to have a million friends. Just try to choose friends who are also good people in your eyes – and be a good friend and person in return.

Your friends can get it very wrong

Sometimes our friends are wrong. Sometimes their side of a story is inaccurate. Sometimes our friends don't relay the whole truth. Sometimes the person they want us to dislike is not someone we should dislike at all. Be loyal to your friendships without following your friends blindly, and when you seek support from friends be accountable and be honest.

Have you ever listened to a friend vent and felt like something just didn't seem right? Maybe you have a friend who always comes to you with very specific complaints about their interactions with other people, but you've realised that the common denominator in all the accounts is your friend? Perhaps you have a friend who can sometimes twist the truth when they recount disputes with others? Maybe you have a friend who struggles with accountability? The thing about friends is that although we care about them and may even love them, they're human – and humans are flawed. No friend is a perfect person and sometimes you may need to evaluate your friendships with this in mind.

A mistake people can make in their friendships is following their friends blindly. It's good to be a supportive friend, but the most supportive friend is not the one who says 'yes' to everything, or the one who agrees with you all the time. The most supportive friend is the one who tells you the truth and holds you accountable in the moments when you may mess up. That said, a great friend has tact and can do all of this in a loving and compassionate way (so please don't use this as an excuse to be 'brutally' honest or, in other words, unkind in your communication).

To be a good friend, we must tell our friends the truth, and this includes telling them when they're wrong. But how do you go about this in the best way? Firstly, you listen. When your friend is sharing a story simply listen until they have vented and said everything they need to say. This will help you – and them – gain clarity. Once they have shared their rendition of events, don't immediately lambast them. Instead, begin to ask them questions to help them unpack their own account of events; for example: 'What triggered that?' 'How did you react?' 'Do you think you handled it in the best way?' Then from there, depending on your own assessment, ask them if they would like some advice. Unsolicited advice in the wrong moment can go down terribly. If they say they wouldn't like advice, hold off until the timing is right. If they would, talk to them kindly about the fact that you want them to be the best version of themselves they can be, but in order for that to happen they may need to reconsider some aspects of their behaviour.

Even constructive feedback can sting. It's not easy to hear that we need to do better, even if it's said in a loving way. But that's partly what good friends are for: assisting us in ways that will contribute to us becoming better people in the future.

Also, in being a good friend yourself, don't expect blind support from your friends, and when you want their opinion on something tell them the whole truth. A good friendship is a two-way street. Like a good romantic relationship, the most fulfilling friendships are those that involve honesty and reciprocation. To maintain good friendships, you also need to be a good friend.

Friends don't always grow at the same pace

> *You'll outgrow some people. Not necessarily because they're on the wrong path, but simply because your paths don't align.*

When it's time for you to evolve, you start feeling uncomfortable. Things that never bothered you before suddenly start to bother you. It's typically a nudge for you to move on to something bigger and better. When this uncomfortable feeling occurs, you may find that your relationships with others begin to feel uncomfortable too.

Have you ever walked away from a friendship, not because the other person actively did something wrong to you, but because you just grew apart? Outgrowing friendships is a common cause of friendship breakdowns. It can also feel very hard to understand, and somewhat frustrating, because we're often used to dealing with relationship breakdowns in a very abrupt and direct way, but a friendship breakdown as a result of growing apart is often slow and steady.

Signs you and a friend may be growing apart:

You feel like you and your friend have less and less in common.
Friendships are commonly formed based on mutual interests and shared values. There's typically something that connects you and the other person; your bond just makes sense. When you're growing apart, however, you'll find that what connected you before no longer connects you. Perhaps you shared a common interest and now one person is disinterested, or maybe you shared values that you no longer share.

You may catch yourself becoming easily irritated by their actions or decisions.
With age, our values can change. What we valued at 18 can be very different to what we value at 28. However, in friendships your values won't always evolve at the same pace. Maybe one person has had a change in values, while the other person is still valuing the same things they did when they were much younger. When

this happens, it's not uncommon for friends to find themselves feeling irritated by one another. This tends to be a result of not feeling comfortable with how each person chooses to live their life.

You may find yourself avoiding communication with them or even making excuses pertaining to why you can't spend time with them.

When you avoid communication with someone, it's usually a sign that something is wrong – particularly when that someone is a person you used to enjoy speaking to regularly. Avoiding conversations can be due to wanting to avoid confrontation – because deep down you know there is an issue at hand that needs to be dealt with. Alternatively, avoiding communication is another way to initiate distance from someone, in the hope that they stop trying to communicate entirely (it's not a good way to handle an issue, though).

It's not strange to outgrow people. You may find yourself feeling like an awful person when this happens, especially if your friend has done nothing malicious to you. But if the company you keep no longer aligns with your mindset, values or principles, sometimes separation is the only option. I will say this, though: if your friend once meant something to you, you owe it to them to communicate how you feel. Ghosting people is never the answer. It's cruel to disappear on people who care about us with no explanation, so if you feel yourself outgrowing a friend, talk to them. In talking to them, you may even discover that the same things that are unsettling your spirit are also unsettling them. You may find that they are experiencing an internal battle with their own life decisions and values, and through all the changes they've been struggling. In speaking to them, you may realise that you don't want to distance yourself after all, but that you just needed to have a heart-to-heart.

If you speak with them and you confirm that you no longer want to maintain the friendship, tell them this without belittling them. As I previously stated, outgrowing people isn't strictly about one person doing better than the other; sometimes it's simply a case of walking different paths. Stress this and mention that you feel like you're going in two different directions.

Sometimes people will exit your life, and you might exit theirs, because your life is about to move in a new direction. Deep down, someone might know that their presence isn't conducive to the direction you're about to go in, and neither of you should feel guilty about that. Creating distance as a result of outgrowing someone also doesn't mean we no longer love them. Sometimes we must choose to love certain friends from afar.

Your support for your friends shouldn't be contingent on you doing better than them

You don't stop supporting your friends when they start doing better than you. If your support is only given on the proviso that they're doing worse than you, then your relationship isn't about love. It's about power and your ego.

Have you ever had a 'friend' who got very salty every time something good happened to you? When I say 'friend', I use the term loosely by the way ... I once had a friend like this. Each time I shared good news or achieved something special there would be a look of disdain on her face. Unlike my other friends, who rejoiced at my wins, this one always had a weird energy around her and gave backhanded compliments when I was at my happiest.

Once upon a time, I used to proclaim that good friends *never* get jealous of their friends. But, in actuality, jealousy is a normal human emotion that people face from time to time. Do I think a good friend can experience jealousy? Yes. But it's what they do in their moments of jealousy that makes the difference. I've had people close to me open up about being jealous of me at times, but it didn't make me think badly of them, because frankly their jealous moments weren't obvious to me. Unlike with my ex-friend who would outwardly show annoyance at me showing joy, my other experiences always involved overwhelming support and care, even if they had a fleeting desire to be in my shoes. I also use the term fleeting to stress the fact that it was exactly that. It was rarely something that was dwelt on and overanalysed, because their love and care for me outweighed any other emotions they may have grappled with. The same is true for me. Admittedly, I've experienced moments where I thought, 'Wow, she's so lucky, I wish I had that,' but they have never been more than a thought that quickly disintegrated and didn't impact my ability to be happy for my friend or celebrate them.

Sadly, not everyone is like this. Some friends want to see you doing well but not better than them. Their relationship with you is centred around their own sense of superiority. Once you challenge that, they no longer have a place for you because they struggle to relate to you when you're exceeding them. Friends like these aren't the type you should have anyway and, frankly, I wouldn't even call them real friends. They often keep you around to stroke their own ego. They like feeling as though they're better than you. When that dynamic is disturbed, they become uninterested and their true colours and feelings for you tend to show.

It's not always easy to see friends surpassing you in certain ways. Perhaps they earn more money than you, have a more exciting career, get more attention than you when you're out together, etc. Whatever it may be, what they have and don't have shouldn't be the deciding factor when it comes to how much you care about them. Your care for them should be based on their character, not where they are in their life compared with where you are in yours. If you were once doing better than them, and no longer are, that's not a reason to stop showing them care and support. Some days they will be doing better, other days you will – and that's life. In your moments of jealousy remind yourself that your friend's happiness will extend to you, and that in itself is something to celebrate.

Time is not the best measure of a good friendship

Sometimes our relationships with others last a long time because someone is compliant, someone is being manipulated, someone is too scared to leave, someone is keeping up appearances. The length of a union isn't always a reflection of its quality. Bad ones can be long too.

This is a public service announcement: your longest friendship isn't necessarily your best one.

When people measure the quality of a bond, time is often used as a marker. I understand why people do this, because after all we're more likely to spend extended periods of time with a good person. But time alone isn't enough.

Have you ever met someone and just bonded with them instantly? When this happens, it doesn't take long to feel like you've known them all your life. Or maybe you've met someone and you've shared more with them in a short space of time than you have with people you've known for a much longer period? Time can be an indicator of friendship quality, but it can also be deceptive. Some friendships last a long time purely because neither party wants to call it quits – not because the friendship is a great one; the average person often feels very loyal to the concept of time, and to a degree I get it. Time is something we cannot get back, so we see it as an 'investment' of sorts.

However, we shouldn't create a habit of prioritising our connections to people solely according to time. Other important factors include how comfortable we feel around them, how similar our values are and whether they truly possess the qualities that make them a good friend. For this reason, we also shouldn't be completely closed off to making new friends, just because we have people in our lives who have been around for several years. In fact, because people don't always grow at the same pace, you may discover when making new friends that you have more in common with them than you do with the friends you've had since you were young – simply because the new connections mirror exactly who you are now, not who you were ten years ago.

But how does one even go about making new friends? Some of the most common places to meet new friends include online, gyms or exercise classes, places of worship (if you're religious), work (if you're comfortable being friends with people you work with), through other existing friends or at social gatherings like parties or ticketed events. If you're looking for like-minded friends, simply visit places *you* would like. In these places, you may have to step out of your comfort zone and make the first move. Introduce yourself, exchange details, extend an invitation to meet up and make an effort to remain connected. Meeting new friends is honestly a bit like dating – but with less pressure. You go where you can meet people, you talk to the person who catches your attention and you invest in getting to know them without the nerve-wracking romantic expectations. If you like what you get to know, you continue to invest in the connection, and if not, you search for other potential friends.

Good friends can be people you've known for ten years, ten months or even ten weeks. Time is not the indicator – character and effort is.

Be wary of people who open up too quickly

One tactic used by emotional manipulators is getting very deep very quickly. They may share 'deep secrets/vulnerabilities' with you, not because they want to build genuine intimacy, but because they need you to let your guard down and feel comfortable enough to let them in ...

One thing I have learned in my life is that, sadly, some people will open up to you because they have ulterior motives. They want to deceive you into feeling comfortable with them, just so they can ask you to open up, in an attempt to get a front-row seat to your trauma. They don't actually care about helping you or consoling you. They just want to know what you've been through, so they can feel better about their own life by hearing the worst parts of yours. Or perhaps they want to know what you've been through so they can use this very thing against you. They may even want you to open up because they need you to feel like you've 'connected' with them on a deep level. This sense of connection enables them to take advantage in some way. They may even lie to you when sharing their own secrets and vulnerabilities … just as long as you believe what they say enough to trust them. They need you to trust their intentions so they can get whatever it is they want from you.

While I haven't experienced something so disheartening first-hand, people close to me have. I remember on one occasion my sister began making a new friend – or so she thought. Getting to know each other began with a series of phone calls – which involved the other young woman opening up quite quickly and quite significantly to my sister. On first impression the young woman appeared very vulnerable, which in turn made my sister feel comfortable about sharing aspects of her own life. My sister was excited and happy to make a new friend, and the other person's vulnerability made my sister very trusting. Following my sister's decision to open up, that same woman never spoke to her again. That entire interaction provided this valuable lesson: not every moment of vulnerability is what it appears to be …

That's not to say all people who open up to you when you're making new friends will have bad intentions.

Plenty won't, and I'm not trying to scare you out of making new connections with people. I just want you to be discerning when making these connections – particularly when people open up rather quickly. Getting to know others naturally is typically a gradual process. Jumping quickly into deep secrets/stories could indicate sinister intentions.

One way to discern whether someone is opening up for support or something darker is to assess whether, if after opening up to you, they prod you to do the same. Are stories about their life followed by: 'So what about you? Have you ever been through that too?' Someone fishing for information following their own personal stories may just want to pry into your life …

People may also confuse manipulators with natural over-sharers. But over-sharers share out of anxiety. They respect your boundaries. You rarely feel like they're prying. They talk a lot about themselves, but it's not often followed by an 'ask' or a push for you to open up as well. Over-sharers aren't looking to use information against you or nudge you to do something you may not typically do. They just want to fill silence, and their body language tends to reflect their anxiety. Emotional manipulators are slicker, more charming, more calculated … Over-sharers do a lot of talking, while people with ulterior motives often ask a lot of questions and want to prompt *you* to do a lot of talking.

Does this mean you shouldn't be vulnerable in a quest to make new friends? Not at all. Just be mindful that anything you say or do you should feel comfortable with. If you don't feel ready to share something – don't. Although time is not a measure of good friends, trust also isn't built overnight.

Friendship break-ups are another type of heartbreak

Friendship break-ups can be much more devastating than romantic ones. Especially when you did almost everything together and imagined that person being there for all your future milestones.

Have you ever walked away from a friendship before? It can be crushing. Society places so much emphasis on romantic break-ups, while underemphasising the effect a friendship break-up can have on our lives, and yet arguably, to plenty of people, friendship break-ups are even worse for a variety of reasons. For one, most of us have come to terms with the fact that the majority of romantic relationships end in a break-up. Unless we choose to spend our life with someone, we will break up with them, and even when we choose to spend our life with them, a break-up can still happen. However, friendships typically outlast romantic relationships.

If you ask a group of people whether their longest friendship boasts more years than their longest relationship, I'm inclined to believe most people will say 'yes'. This is partly why friendship break-ups can be so painful. When you spend many years with someone, you collect a vast array of memories together, which include plenty of shared experiences. You would have shared so much of your life with them and discussed so much of your 'future' life. When it comes to our closest of friends, there are things we cannot imagine doing without them. For example, I can't imagine getting married and not having my best friend around, or not being there for her special day. I can't imagine us having children and not sharing these experiences with each other. Even the thought of it now makes my heart ache.

Admittedly, there is no eye-opening lesson here, but rather an acknowledgement that friendships can cause heartbreak too. Heartbreak is not reserved for romantic connections alone. It is the result of lost or damaged love, and we are very capable of loving our friends just as much as we love our romantic partners – and sometimes even more, just in a different way.

So if you experience a friendship break-up, give yourself the time to grieve. It doesn't matter who breaks our heart – just that our heart is broken. When we lose a close friend, it can feel like we have lost a part of ourselves. The compassion we give to ourselves after a romantic heartbreak should be applied to the loss of a friendship too.

The pain people cause us doesn't always impact their happiness

You may see people who have hurt you go on to live happy lives (on the surface). Whether they succeed or appear happy shouldn't concern you. You may be waiting on karma, but don't wait forever. Don't allow them to inhabit your mind. Give yourself permission to move on …

Karma is a Sanskrit word meaning 'action'. The term is often defined as 'the sum of a person's actions in this and previous states of existence, viewed as deciding their fate in future existences'. If you've ever been deeply hurt by someone, and you don't feel as if they have dealt with any repercussions, you may have hoped that karma would swoop in eventually, rebalancing the universe by righting their wrongs.

The thing about repercussions is that they don't always occur the way we want them to, and sometimes the villains in our story don't always see the ending we would like. Do I believe in karma? To a degree. I do not believe karma to be an obvious and direct spiritual intervention in the way some people do. My own interpretation of karma is more in line with the literal Sanskrit meaning – 'action'. I believe that every action has a reaction, and in everything we do there will be a consequence – whether minor or significant, positive or negative. However, that consequence is not always predictable. So, sadly, sometimes people may carry out bad actions and see results they would deem as positive.

When we see this happening in our own lives, we can't allow it to consume us. What's often best is moving forward and letting go of resentment completely. As much as it may sting to see the person who hurt us appear happy, remember that you deserve to be happy too. And that's hard to do if you're constantly comparing your life to theirs, or if you're wrapped up in negative emotions, waiting for them to feel the hurt they caused you. They may never feel it in a direct and obvious way, but that shouldn't disrupt your healing and feed resentment. They say holding on to resentment is like drinking poison and hoping it will kill your enemies. Sometimes forgiving others for causing us hurt is a gift to us, not them.

Your romantic relationships shouldn't replace your friendships

> *No matter how great you think your romantic relationship is, there is a space only your platonic friends can fill. Recognise this and don't abandon your greatest friends for love.*

I'm going to make an assumption here, which is that your closest friendship has outlasted the majority of your romantic connections. I'm making this assumption because it is true for the majority of people. Relationships come and go, and friendships ... well ... they can come and go too, but typically not as regularly. Yet despite this, plenty of people (particularly young women) make the mistake of prioritising their romantic relationship to the detriment of their friendships at some point in their life.

I remember my first serious relationship. I was so excited by the thrill of it all that I completely misman-aged my free time. I invested the majority of it in the relationship, while overlooking the friendships I'd formed before that relationship existed. When people make the mistake I made, it's usually not intentional. They just get so engulfed by the new feelings and experiences they are enjoying with their new partner that they sometimes forget about the people who were already in their life before they appeared. And for many, it's not something that is asked of us by our partner. Sure, some people may find themselves with partners who intentionally try to isolate them (which is an abuse tactic), but other people indirectly isolate themselves. For others still, it may even be directly, based on the personal belief that this is what you're supposed to do when you're in a relationship. If you get into the routine of abandoning your friends every time you have a new relationship, you will find yourself in a painful situation if the relationship ends (and most do) – having no one to turn to in heartbreak, while attempting to rebuild the friendships you once had.

The thing is, romantic love doesn't replace friendship – and shouldn't. The connection most people have with their greatest friend is unlike the connection they have with their partner. Can your partner be your best friend? Most certainly, and one can only strive for that type of connection. But that doesn't mean your other friends should cease to exist. The genuine and healthy friend-ships we discover outside of romance are friendships that aren't impacted by a sense of romantic duty. They're not friendships where physical intimacy is a core part of your connection. They're not friendships that rely on the presence of romantic feelings or attraction.

Friends offer a different type of love. There are things you may want to talk to friends about that you may not want to talk to your romantic partner about. This doesn't automatically mean you are hiding things of significance, but rather that friendships can operate in a different way. Friendships can also bring balance to our lives. In my debut book I wrote about how your partner shouldn't be your life – and it's true. A romantic rela-tionship should complement the life you already have, and this includes your friendships.

Your friends and your partner should be able to co-exist in your life. Always.

Section 3:
Making the Most
Out of Your Career

This section of my book covers the lessons I learned that have helped me reach my goals and make the most out of my career. Prior to being a writer and creator, the jobs I had in my teens and twenties included being a receptionist, retail assistant, student mentor, business utilities executive, PR assistant, digital media manager, communications manager, and more! In each job I learned something new, which widened my skillset and brought me even closer to determining what I wanted to get out of my career. Did I enjoy every job? No. In fact, I hated some of them. But my dislike didn't negate the fact that even during hard times I learned valuable lessons.

One of my worst experiences was as a PR assistant in a small public relations company. The job itself wasn't particularly hard or complex, but my line manager at the time was awful to me. While I worked there, I struggled to sleep due to the debilitating anxiety I experienced, so I felt constantly exhausted. There would even be days when I would go home and burst into tears because of how I was treated. As awful as that specific job was, one thing it taught me was that who you work with can make or break your experience. In fact, who you work with can make a mundane job a great one or a great opportunity an excruciating one. One of my more enjoyable jobs included working for the UK's National Health Service as a digital media manager. It was a job that allowed me to exercise my strengths, exhibit creativity and help people in the process. I guess you could say that it emphasised how much I enjoy social media and having the opportunity to make a difference in people's lives.

I'm in a great place now work-wise. I love my job and couldn't imagine doing anything else. But I didn't get to this place overnight. It took a lot of job trial and error, faith in myself, and a willingness to try something new and take risks. I'm hoping that by the time you finish this section of my book, you will feel more confident about making the most out of your career.

Success lies outside of your comfort zone

Often, the only thing standing in between most people and their success story is a willingness to step out of their comfort zone. If you want to build a life that fulfils you, you're going to have to take risks or do things that challenge you.

If you've read *I Wish I Knew This Earlier: Lessons on Love*, you'll know how passionate I am about stepping out of your comfort zone. In that book, I touched on the topic in relation to romantic love and helped readers through the idea that sometimes our relationship comfort zones aren't always healthy. This time, I want to focus on the importance of stepping out of your comfort zone more generally.

One fact about me that people are often surprised by is that I used to hate public speaking – so much so that in my twenties I turned down numerous paid opportunities to host events just because I was too scared to get on stage. Talking in front of crowds was way out of my comfort zone, and as a result I blocked a lot of personal blessings because I refused to challenge myself. People are so surprised by this fact because public speaking is now a major aspect of my career. To date, I have been paid to speak for the likes of J.P. Morgan, Ernst & Young, Samsung, Bumble and many more, and I'm proud to say I'm no longer frightened by the prospect of speaking in front of crowds.

Now, at this point you're probably thinking, 'How did you muster the courage to face stepping out of your comfort zone?' All will be revealed. But before I do that, I first want to outline what your comfort zone is, and why stepping out of it is so important.

The term 'comfort zone' was originally coined by business management theorist Alasdair White in 2009. It is often described as 'a psychological state in which things feel familiar to a person and they are at ease and in control of their environment, experiencing low levels of anxiety and stress' – or, more literally, a state of comfort. Since the term was coined, many psychologists, theorists and thought leaders have stressed the importance of stepping out of your comfort zone – but the value in doing so is a belief that is far from new. In the first half of the 1900s, Harvard University animal behaviourists Robert Mearns Yerkes and John Dillingham Dodson proposed the Yerkes–Dodson Law, after a series of experiments. This law theorised that optimising performance required a slightly higher level of stress – referred to as 'optimal anxiety'. According to Yerkes, 'Anxiety improves performance until a certain optimum level of arousal has been reached. Beyond that point, performance deteriorates as higher levels of anxiety are attained.'*

So what can we deduce from that? Performance is improved when we take risks – but risk management is also important. So how does one take risks while also ensuring you don't reach higher levels of anxiety that could be damaging? One way to do this is to take small steps. People can make the mistake of believing stepping out of your comfort zone involves making a single massive change, but this isn't necessarily true. Incremental change can be just as effective. When I was still scared of public speaking, I decided to take small

* R M Yerkes, J D Dodson, 'The relationship of strength of stimulus to rapidity of habit formation', Journal of Comparative Neurology and Psychology, 1908.

steps towards feeling more comfortable. Step one involved attending talks as a guest and hearing other people speak; step two involved attending courses on how to be a more confident speaker, and step three involved saying 'yes' when I wanted to say 'no'.

One thing about me is that I hate disappointing people, so, personally, my worries about being seen as unreliable trumped my concerns about public speaking. In my mind, if I said yes, I couldn't back out. The first time I said yes was for a small panel discussion in 2018. I was so anxious on the day, but I showed up because I didn't want to be the one person who didn't follow through. As I started receiving questions, I felt extremely nervous and would catch myself stuttering or mumbling my words. Once some minutes had passed, the stuttering reduced and I soon discovered that, although I was nervous, the picture I had put together in my head prior to speaking was ten times worse. I came to learn that the fear of stepping out of my comfort zone exaggerated the potential issues that could arise from stepping into something new. I was so grateful that I had taken those small and incremental steps to get to where I was.

Another way to step out of your comfort zone while also managing your anxiety levels is to take calculated risks. In 2020, during the height of the coronavirus pandemic, I left my nine-to-five job to pursue writing and content creation full time. During this period, people around me thought I was insane. As far as my manager, some of my family members and some select friends were concerned, leaving a position of security in a time of unpredictability was a massive risk. What many didn't realise at the time was that my decision was not one made on a whim. I had prepared and put in a lot of assessment hours to determine whether the choice I was making was a good one. At the time, I had money put aside in savings. This pot was one that I had been building for a year, because I knew that my goal was to work for myself eventually. Additionally, I had already been approached to write *I Wish I Knew This Earlier*, so I knew I could expect a book advance by the end of the year – although I didn't know how much it would be at the time. So, for extra security, I mapped out my cost of living against the savings I had and deduced that if I didn't make a single penny from working for myself, I could afford to be 'jobless' for six months. But I knew I was going to make *something* from my book, and my content wasn't that bad that I wouldn't make a single penny for six months – so as far as I was concerned, me leaving my job wasn't a huge risk. In my mind, I could afford to be out of work for a year. As someone who is generally quite risk adverse, I am a big advocate of calculated risks because they allow you to step out of your comfort zone while still retaining an element of control.

Another thing I recommend to assist you in stepping out of your comfort zone is expanding your social circle or leaving your typical 'social bubble' sometimes. Beyond your city, beyond your usual 'type' of friends, beyond the places you usually frequent, there's so much more to discover. So much more that will contribute to your growth and open your views. You may be thinking that expanding your network is stepping out of your comfort zone in itself – and you're right. So do it incrementally and take calculated risks. Ease yourself into unfamiliar spaces and gradually increase your degrees of separation to people. Once you get into the swing of expanding your social bubble, you will soon learn more about others, and discover that what is daunting to you is 'normal' to another person, and vice versa.

I'm currently living like a bit of a nomad: I moved out of my London apartment to travel as much as I can this year, but prior to living in London, I lived in Oxfordshire and would spend a lot of time in London to socialise and work – having also attended university in the city, despite Oxford Brookes being my parents' first choice for me. Despite being just two hours away from one another, London and Oxfordshire are very different … but their differences contributed to my growth in a way I'm so grateful for. I genuinely believe that if I'd never studied outside of my hometown and subsequently socialised and worked in a big city, I wouldn't be working for myself now, doing what I love. I wouldn't have met the people who facilitated this. I wouldn't have networked in the same way.

It's easy to always want to do what feels comfortable. To stay in locations that make us feel at home, to speak to people we can relate to, to take on opportunities that don't feel scary. That's normal, but sometimes it pays to do the opposite.

You may be thinking, 'But what if it doesn't work out?' Well … then it doesn't work out! Why should the potential for failure in the future prevent someone from exploring the possibilities in the moment? Always believe that doors will open for you, even when it feels like they keep closing. If you don't get the outcome you desire from stepping out of your comfort zone, always try again – and remember that trying something new and expanding your horizons will always contribute to your growth.

If you're still worried about stepping out of your comfort zone, remember something very simple: the regret you might feel from failing will never exceed the regret associated with never trying. And failing just brings you one step closer to doing things right, because you now know what not to do next time.

Drown out the naysayers and follow your dreams

It is far easier to criticise the work of others than it is to produce work. It is far easier to ridicule someone else's dreams than to follow your own. Remember this the next time someone mocks the dreams and goals you have for yourself. They're taking the easy route by watching and judging, while you're doing.

When I was still in the early days of growing my online platform (specifically Twitter), I would regularly face criticism from my peers. Statements people often made revolved around me 'writing too much' or not 'shutting up'. A lot of my writing focused on love and relationships, and because I was single at the time it wasn't uncommon for me to be told to 'heal' or to stop talking about relationships altogether – 'It's enough,' they would say. There was one day in 2017 that was very difficult for me. I wrote a long Twitter thread about reasons why women shouldn't pay attention to what men have to say about their physical preferences in them. I didn't insult anyone, belittle anyone or single anyone out – but that was enough for the online bullying to ensue. At first it was a handful of nasty comments, which turned into several, which turned into hundreds.

I'm not sure if you've ever had hundreds of people bashing you simultaneously at once, but it's horrible – especially when you're being criticised for something that wasn't even malicious. The theme of that day was that I write too much on Twitter, and my threads were always too long. I was dubbed 'Threadie Kruger' – which is hilarious to me now, but at the time, not so much. I remember being on the cusp of tears and feeling ready to quit writing online altogether. I started to internalise all those tweets and tell myself things like, 'Maybe I *do* write too much,' 'Maybe I *should* shut up,' 'Maybe I *should* just deactivate my account.' I typically don't seek out help when I'm annoyed, but I was beyond annoyed – I was feeling completely and utterly dejected. I ended up speaking to my mother, who urged me to continue. 'Think of all the people who love your content. You can't let a few idiots ruin this for you,' she said. In hindsight, I am so thankful for her support and encouragement. Instead of deactivating my account, I ended up blocking hundreds of people that day and taking a break to let all the laughs at my expense die down.

During that break, I learned three valuable lessons. The first is that, sadly, some people have a bully's spirit and don't even realise it. They're good at hiding it, and performing, but every so often the mask slips and their true nature emerges. They rarely show grace to their peers. They love a group bashing and will be front and centre when an opportunity to dogpile arises. And then their inner bully comes out. This became clear to me because some of the people who engaged in the online ridicule that day were people who I thought enjoyed my content – because they followed me, interacted with me and for the most part seemed quite nice. But as covert bullies will do; when the chance arises to pick on someone as part of a collective, they joined in.

The second lesson I learned is that although people suggest negative voices are often the loudest, that's not always true. Typically, people just pay less attention to the positive ones. For all the mockery or nasty tweets at my expense, there were just as many kind and supportive ones. Even prior to that fateful day in 2017, I'd received many messages of support from people who had told me my content had helped them in ways I couldn't even fathom. I had almost forgotten about all the good feedback; so much so that I was close to quitting because of the bad feedback.

The third lesson I learned was that I cannot let other people's criticisms disrupt the dreams and hopes I have for myself. You will never impress everybody; you will never be liked by everybody; not everyone will understand your passions. But if you have a goal for yourself or if you are pursuing a purpose, that should always take precedence. Fast forward to today, and I'm a bestselling author with two books under my belt. If I had listened to all the people who told me to shut up, I wouldn't have my dream career, nor would I be living my dream life. The irony in all of this is that the majority of those same people are still on Twitter doing what they do best: criticising other people, instead of investing their energy in their own lives. So, take that as a fourth lesson if you will. Don't be the person who criticises other people for being brave enough to chase their dreams. Be the person who chases their own dreams.

Overworking yourself isn't a measure of success – nobody wins medals for burnout

> *It's a common misconception that reaching your goals requires overworking. This isn't true. You don't have to work until you burn out. Simply have a goal in mind, remain consistent, and make the most of the tools and the people you have access to who can help you gain big results with small steps.*

Have you ever heard the phrase 'Work smarter, not harder'? It is a quote attributed to Allen F. Morgenstern, an industrial engineer, in the 1930s, and it has stuck with me throughout my life. In fact, in all that I do I try not to exert myself. Does this mean I don't work 'hard'? Well, it depends on how you define hard work. I work, but not in a way that involves burning out or doing a lot in exchange for a little. I'm results led. When it comes to my career, I care less about the mountains I have to climb and the rivers I have to cross to get to the finish line. I care more about simply getting to the finish line as comfortably as possible.

Here are a few of my tips for working 'smarter':

Make the most of quick wins that have high impact.

During my early corporate days, I often felt overwhelmed by the sheer number of tasks I had to carry out on a weekly or even daily basis. At times, I felt like the workload I had didn't even tally up to the number of hours I had in a day, so being strategic with my to-do list was very important. Rather than try to accomplish absolutely everything, I would break down my list according to what was 'easy' to accomplish, what had an impending deadline and what would yield the greatest results (e.g. a task that was very important to a senior member of staff). That way, I was less preoccupied about doing *everything* on my list; rather I prioritised the vital and 'easy' stuff. In the words of author and speaker Brian Tracy: 'There is never enough time to do everything, but there is always enough time to do the most important thing.'* One

---

* Brian Tracy, 'The 100 Absolutely Unbreakable Laws of Business Success', 2002.

thing I learned from this is that even when you're in a job that requires you to do a hundred things in a day, the people you are accountable to don't actually care about the hundred things – just the ones that have a significant impact if they're not done on time.

Delegate, ask for support and bring in experts.

Sometimes you have to 'let the plumbers do the plumbing'. What do I mean by that? There will be people who have the skills to carry out the task you need completed. Utilise them. Don't attempt to be an expert at absolutely everything because, frankly, that's tiring and pretty impossible. Instead, work to your strengths, and when you notice a weakness, delegate if you can or ask an expert for advice and guidance.

Take breaks.

You may be thinking, 'How does this help me work smart?' Well, on a very basic level, the better you feel, the more productive you are. Staying up throughout the night to work is only going to leave you tired the following day. Skipping meals to work is only going to leave you low in energy. Take time out to recharge, refuel and reset. I take regular breaks, and my creativity is always better for it.

If you don't have to invest a lot of time, then don't.
Digital tools are my best friend. Especially when it comes to working smart. Whether it's web templates, digital libraries, automated spreadsheets, artificial intelligence and more. If I can download an app that will make my work life easier, or get a gadget that will improve my productivity, then I will. After all, digital tools and tech are there to help us, so if you have access to these options and can use them to save time, then do it.

Now I'm not saying you should cheat your way into working smart. As much as I'm big on seeing results and getting the job done with ease, also work with integrity. Don't lie or steal when it comes to the work you deliver. Just remember, there's a difference between being busy, and being productive.

Discipline is an essential part of success

A lack of discipline is a very easy way to crush all your potential. Many people are capable of achieving great things, but they're not disciplined enough to focus, prioritise or say no to certain temptations. They always give in to distractions, and that's what hurts them ...

Sometimes the only thing standing in between you and your success is your ability to focus and prioritise. The end result is reachable, but you're procrastinating and you're distracted.

For the first half of my twenties, I was disciplined in my personal life, but not as disciplined with my work. I struggled to be consistent when creating content and would often find myself easily distracted, moving on to a brand-new venture when I wasn't seeing the results I wanted. But at some point I had to ask myself a very simple question:

*'Is the way I'm choosing to live my life
now conducive to the kind of life
I want in the future?'*

Discipline contributes to success of every type. Whether that's career success, relationship success or simply having a healthy lifestyle. Be disciplined enough to remain consistent, disciplined enough to fight temptation and disciplined enough to give it your all. Below are six ways to improve discipline in your life:

1. Affirm your goals. Write them down and put them where you can see them. This acts as a reminder of why you're trying to be disciplined in the first place.
2. Set small, achievable, realistic goals initially. It's easy to lose discipline when you're faced with mammoth tasks. As you achieve a small thing, work your way up.
3. Remove temptations. You might be tempted by certain things, or it could even be people who distract you from your purpose or goal. It's much easier to give in to these

distractions when they're within reach. Do your best to remove them if you can or create distance.

4. Form new habits that encourage and instil discipline, like making your bed in the morning, meditating every day or even taking a walk. You'd be surprised at how these daily rituals help to create structure in other aspects of your life.

5. Stop people-pleasing. Sometimes a lack of discipline isn't even due to giving into temptations. It could be the result of an inability to say no to people because you're trying to please everyone. You only have one life to live. Self-prioritise when necessary.

6. Forgive yourself for failing. If you give in to temptation and then beat yourself up over that one mistake, it's easy to quit altogether. But people do make mistakes. Pick yourself up and try again.

Improving discipline is an investment in the future. You may not see changes overnight, but the more you make the effort to remain focused, consistent and aligned with your goals, the more you will see results.

Learn to find peace in the 'in between'

> *Don't put pressure on yourself to always have something lined up. Whether it's a project, a job, a trip, a relationship ... Constantly worrying about what's next feeds anxiety. Use the time in between to recoup, reflect and relax so you're ready for what comes, when it comes.*

The year 2021 was a defining one for me career-wise. My first book was published and I became a bestselling author, I was the face of a nationally promoted podcast and I had wrapped up a docuseries with my family. However, as the year was nearing its end, I didn't feel accomplished. Oddly, I felt extremely anxious. Instead of sitting in my successes and allowing myself to bask in them, I allowed them to intimidate me and they quickly turned into a burden. 'How the hell am I going to top this?' I thought. 'Surely, it's only downhill from here ...' I felt as if everything was going to disappear in the blink of an eye, and I was pushing myself to try to figure out what I could do next to maintain a certain trajectory.

I was in a state of panic, and it was debilitating. I'd be anxious during the day, and I'd find myself waking up in the middle of the night in a weird state of discomfort. I'd be checking my bank account religiously, contemplating what I'd do if I couldn't get work again. I'd pressure myself daily, forcing myself to think of new ways to create content. Meanwhile, from the outside looking in, my life was going swimmingly; to other people I looked like I had cracked the code to life.

That's one thing about success that people don't often talk about. While it is wonderful in so many ways, it also comes with its own set of challenges – one of them being an immense sense of pressure. Pressure to live up to other people's expectations of you, pressure to live up to your own expectations of yourself, pressure to deliver, pressure to do better than you did yesterday, pressure to provide, and more. I felt so under pressure after achieving everything I had achieved that part of me just wanted to stop altogether.

That's when I realised I was doing something very dangerous. Part of this pressure I felt was a result of attaching my personal sense of value and self-worth to my newfound achievements. Prior to this life-changing year, I assigned my value to simply being me – a living, breathing human being, worthy of life. After these successes, I started associating my value with my work. And in doing so, I subconsciously told myself that if I am no longer achieving in my career, I will cease to be valuable.

Completing a task, reaching a goal or hitting a milestone is a bit like running a marathon. Once you reach the finish line, one of the worst things you can do is attempt to run another race. Instead, what should you do? You should acknowledge your achievement and take some time to recover. In acknowledging your achievement, you gain a stronger appreciation for the task you carried out. And in taking the time out to recover, you top up the mental fortitude and physical strength you require to eventually run another day. Unfortunately, during my times of anxiety I wasn't basking in my achievements or regenerating. Instead, I was pressuring myself to run another race.

Eventually, I had to remind myself that the quality of my work is more important than taking on work back-to-back. I needed to take time out to be the best version of myself, which would enable me to deliver the best type of work I could. Additionally, even if after taking time out to recuperate there was nothing immediately lined up, I had to tell myself that was okay. It was okay because I am not my achievements. My value to society isn't just about what I can do in my career, and therefore my career highlights do not validate my existence.

So, if you ever have feelings of being bothered by what comes next, remember that you deserve to enjoy the fruits of your labours, to sit in your successes and to relax during those 'in between' moments.

Ask for what you want

> *If you go through life only ever accepting what people want to give you, you'll be dissatisfied, because many people will give you less than you deserve. Don't talk yourself into accepting the bare minimum because you're too nervous to ask. Go for it.*

Once upon a time I used to hate asking for what I wanted. I'd get jobs and accept base salary even when I knew I was worth more. I wouldn't ask for pay increases because I was worried I'd cause offence. In romantic relationships it was the same. I'd rarely ask for what I desired.

Then I realised something. The people I saw as successful and fulfilled were direct about their wants. I was seeing people live the type of life I wanted, and I noticed they didn't shy away from asking for things. They knew that for the most part the worst that could happen was hearing a 'no'. Deep down I knew that too, but I think my fear of rejection and my desire to be viewed as undemanding was so strong that a 'no' from certain people seemed like the end of the world …

Eventually it got to a point where I had to ask myself this question: 'Do I want to create the life I want or do I want to live the life that is handed to me?' I was tired of bending and twisting to suit everyone else. I wanted to stand firm. It was time for me to demand more!

At this point I was still unlearning certain habits, so I had to take on asking for things in stages. It began with asking for small things – such as asking my manager for five extra minutes to run an errand on my lunch break or asking a friend to help me with a chore. Small asks had a high probability of being accepted fuss-free. I needed to know I could be successful. Also, seeing that being brave enough to ask came with immediate benefits also made me feel more confident asking.

Another thing I did was start to ask in writing. For me, this was less pressurised than asking in person because I didn't have to look people in the eye and potentially deal with face-to-face rejection. Arguably, fear of rejection is one of the main reasons people don't ask for what they want. Most people are scared of hearing 'no'. If that's you, consider one thing: should someone reject your ask, how would you want them to tell you? While I prefer in writing, for you it may be the exact opposite. You may feel anxious waiting on written responses and much prefer asking in person. Whatever works for you best, start with that.

Additionally, as I asked for things I would make incremental increases with each request – particularly when I got comfortable asking for higher salaries at new jobs. For example, the first time you ask for a higher starting salary, you might try to round it up with £3,000 extra. The second time, you might ask for £5,000 more, the third time you might request £10,000, and so on. The more you ask, the more you will feel comfortable with asking.

Eventually, for me, asking questions that I previously dreaded became natural. By the time I got into the swing of working for myself, I stopped quivering at the thought of asking someone what their budget was, whether I could change my deliverables or if they could double or triple my fee. It took time, but I got there.

A lesson: nine times out of ten, people initially offer less than they're capable of giving! I have heard more yeses from asking than nos, because there's usually more to give. You just have to be brave enough to ask. Does this mean you should take advantage? Not at all. I don't ask for things that I think someone will be uncomfortable giving or shouldn't give. If I've asked, it's because I think it's possible, and I can offer a justified reason why it should be provided. As long as you can tick these two boxes, ask away!

Be your own cheerleader

> *There are so many people doing amazing work who don't shout about themselves. One thing I've learned in this life is that you need to be your biggest advocate. Women in particular have been led to believe we must be quiet and modest, but it hurts our careers more than it helps us.*

One thing about me: I'm going to shout about myself. I'm the woman who reshares her own content, who is loud about her wins and who shares her career achievements. This ability is one I developed over time, and it has helped me so much. My willingness to share my skills and speak up for myself has allowed my work to be noticed by people who ordinarily might not have encountered it. In fact, my loudness about my work was exactly how I attained my first book deal. I didn't go to the publisher. The publisher came to me. They came to me because they saw me, and they saw me because I was – and still am – my biggest cheerleader.

I once read about an internal Hewlett Packard report, which suggested that women working within the organisation only went for a promotion when they believed they met 100 per cent of the specified qualifications.* Men, however, typically applied when they met roughly 60 per cent of the job specification. A separate Cornell University study found that men overestimate their abilities and performance, while women typically underestimate both.† Sadly, many women downplay their skills, talents and accolades. Plenty of women have been led to believe that to be a woman is to be meek and mild-mannered. What some view as confidence in men is seen as conceitedness in women. What some see as assertiveness in men is seen as bossy in women. So what do some women do? They try to tone down their strengths.

The reason why I stopped myself from doing that is because I noticed one very simple and obvious thing. The people around me who were attracting opportuni-

---

* Deborah L Rhode, Women and Leadership, 2017.

† Tracy Packiam Alloway Ph.D, 'Think Like a Girl: 10 Unique Strengths of a Woman's Brain and How to Make Them Work for You', 2021.

ties were often also the people who would be vocal about what they were working on – which makes a lot of sense. How are people supposed to reward you for your work, or offer you more work, if they don't even know where your skills lie or what you're working on in the first place?!

Some people don't shout about themselves, under the impression that other people should always shout for them. But my question is why? Why should other people believe in you, and be vocal about liking your work, if *you* aren't vocal about liking your work? Being your own cheerleader doesn't have to involve spamming everyone who knows you with endless newsletters and unsolicited updates – just learn to share your career highs.

People might say, 'But it's good to keep things private.' My question in response to this would be, 'But what has your privacy done for you?' I understand career privacy when you're in developmental stages or important details haven't yet been confirmed, but from experience I would say that being loud and proud helps businesses way more than being the opposite.

Money isn't everything

> *Money is an important part of life. After all, most of us need it purely to survive. But when it comes to our careers, there are so many other important factors to consider. Do you feel fulfilled in your job? Do you have a good work–life balance? Does the job align with your values? Do you feel safe at work? Receiving good money is a plus, but not if it comes at the cost of your integrity or peace of mind.*

There are some jobs and opportunities I would never accept, no matter how good the pay might seem. In fact, I've turned down high-paying jobs and opportunities purely because the money being offered wasn't enough to justify all that I would lose in saying 'yes'. For example, I've been offered money to promote fad diet products or products that clearly don't work for people. I've been offered large sums of money for jobs that come with insane working hours, or jobs that I just know I won't be happy in. At the end of the day, my integrity and my sense of peace meant so much more to me than what I could have been paid.

I've also seen second-hand how choosing money over everything can have a massive negative impact on the mental health, physical health and overall happiness of people close to me. I've seen them earning six figures for working six days a week, twelve hours a day, with little to no time off. I've seen them miss important events, sacrifice time with their families and give up their passions, purely for 'the money'. But what use is money if you don't have the time to spend it or enjoy it? And what use is money if you sacrifice everything else that is dear to you?

Before I go further, I acknowledge that being able to say 'money isn't everything' comes from a place of privilege. I know that some people simply don't have much of a choice. They can't afford to be picky with work because of the lack of opportunities they have access to, coupled with the responsibilities they have. They may not always have the job they want, but they get the job that pays the bills.

That said, outside of this cohort of people there are many who have access to an array of different opportunities – in alternative organisations, alternative locations or even varying industries. But they chase the money over everything. Money certainly has its place in society, and having large sums of it can make your life much easier, but I learned that, for me, it's not worth diminishing my freedom, health, peace or creativity for.

Bronnie Ware is an author and speaker best known for her book *The Top Five Regrets of the Dying* – penned from her time as a palliative carer. In her book, Ware outlines the top-five key regrets most people have on their death bed. They are:

- I wish I'd had the courage to live a life true to myself, not the life others expected of me.
- I wish I hadn't worked so hard.
- I wish I'd had the courage to express my feelings.
- I wish I'd stayed in touch with friends.
- I wish that I had let myself be happier.

Notice how none of the top regrets include 'I wish I made more money'? In fact, the only work-related regret is wishing they didn't work so hard!

What do these regrets tell you? While I can't speak for you, they tell me that being true to yourself, and prioritising your relationships and happiness, is worth more than anything else – even money.

Social media is as real as you and me

Plenty of people say 'social media isn't real life' as a way to excuse bad behaviour. This is part of the problem. People will justify bullying others online, lying online, cheating online or compromising their entire character, as if there are no real consequences.

As someone who has amassed a large social media following, and who has done a decent job of staying out of trouble (for the most part), one piece of advice I want to give to you is that social media is indeed very real. While there are things on social media that are false, exaggerated or inaccurate, there's lots online that is not. Behind many profiles are real people, with real lives, real connections and real feelings. There's also a footprint for everything. Even when you think you're hiding, you're not.

I've seen first-hand what can happen to people who treat social media as if it's some fictional vortex where repercussions simply don't exist. In my opinion, separating social media from reality does more harm than good – and it has got many people in trouble. I've seen people lose jobs, opportunities, their reputation and even their relationship, all because of how they chose to utilise their online platforms.

We live in a digital age, and whether we like it or not social media has become an extension of our reality. Be mindful of this when you engage with people online, and also be mindful of how you choose to carry yourself in the online space. How do people view you in person, and how do you want them to view you online? How do you communicate with people in person, and how do you wish to maintain communication online? Which values do you live by in person and which values do you want to live by online? While your online profile may not mirror your in-person persona perfectly, the two are conjoined.

I say this because social media is a fantastic tool when used properly. And by properly, I don't mean that every user needs to do what I did and build a career from their online presence. By properly, I mean 'used in a way that contributes to your wellbeing' – whether that's through entertaining you, making you laugh, building new connections, making a living or learning something new.

Like many things, much of what you get out of social media is guided by what you put into it. Here are three tips from me for making the most out of your online experiences:

- Follow accounts that align with what you're trying to get out of your online presence. For example, if you are struggling with your physical confidence, follow body-confidence coaches, rather than people and pages who encourage you to feel bad about the way you look.
- Build a page that reflects the image you want to portray. If you're using socials for business, consider the type of content you put out and how it could impact the income you generate. If you're using socials for personal reasons, consider how much you're actually comfortable sharing online – with the understanding that what is online is never truly 'private'.
- Participate in feel-good conversations. Being angry online all the time is not going to contribute to an enjoyable social-media

experience. You have the choice to engage in certain conversations and disengage from others. Be particular when it comes not just to who you talk to, but how you talk to them.

Remember, while social media may not feel real, it produces very real results – so maximise your results.

Conclusion

To conclude, I truly believe that a large part of living a happier and more fulfilling life is through taking in all the real lessons that life has to offer. Growing up, I had a lot of questions. In fact, I still do, but my growth through the years is a product of asking myself one of the most important questions of all: 'What do I have to learn from this?' – and asking that question has enabled me to work towards reaching my full potential.

In everything we do there is a lesson, and answers often emerge when we're willing to learn from every failure, every success, every friendship, every crossroads, every area of doubt, every negative emotion and every positive one.

I sincerely hope there is something you can take away from *Take Note*, and that my real life lessons have proved valuable to you. I hope you put this book down with a greater sense of identity, a stronger sense of confidence and a firmer sense of purpose. I hope you walk away feeling more empowered in your friendships, and with a better understanding of what you want from your friends, how to be a better friend yourself and the value of support systems. I hope you approach your career goals feeling more inspired to take risks, to ask for what you want and to work more holistically. I hope, all in all, this book makes a change in at least one aspect of your life – but hopefully across all three: your identity, your friendships and your career.

In your journey towards living to your full potential, please show yourself grace. Please show yourself compassion. Remember that 'comparison is the thief of joy', and that the journey you are on is unique to you. Remember that nobody can define your life more than you can – and your future is a result of your thoughts, your actions and your efforts. Your life is in your hands, and you should tailor it according to how you see fit – not according to what people expect of you.

If there is anything you wish to expand on, let's keep the lessons going. I'll always be on the lookout for more lessons or for your thoughts on mine, so please share – #TakeNoteLessons.

Toni